CZECH REPUBLIC 2016 HUMAN RIGHTS REPORT

EXECUTIVE SUMMARY

Czech Republic is a multiparty parliamentary democracy. Legislative authority is vested in a bicameral parliament, consisting of a Chamber of Deputies (Poslanecka snemovna) and the senate (Senat). The president is head of state and appoints a prime minister from the majority party or coalition. In 2013 voters elected Milos Zeman to a five-year term as president in the country's first direct presidential election. On October 7 and 8, the country held senate and regional elections. Observers considered the elections free and fair.

Civilian authorities maintained effective control over the security forces.

Societal discrimination against the Romani population in education, housing, and employment remained a serious problem. With the continuing influx of refugees and migrants to Europe from mostly Muslim countries, including Syria, Iraq, Afghanistan, and Eritrea, and domestic political opposition to resettlement of those refugees in the country, anti-immigrant and anti-Muslim sentiment continued during the year. There were no reports of egregious human rights abuses.

Other human rights problems included prison overcrowding; police corruption; inflammatory speech by politicians and public figures; long detention of migrants and asylum seekers; violence against women; sexual and other abuse of children; anti-Semitism; trafficking in persons; discrimination against persons with HIV/AIDS; and exploitation of migrant workers.

The government took steps to prosecute and punish officials who committed abuses in the security services and elsewhere in the government.

Section 1. Respect for the Integrity of the Person, Including Freedom from:

a. Arbitrary Deprivation of Life and other Unlawful or Politically Motivated Killings

There were no reports that the government or its agents committed arbitrary or unlawful killings.

b. Disappearance

There were no reports of politically motivated disappearances.

c. Torture and Other Cruel, Inhuman, or Degrading Treatment or Punishment

The law prohibits such practices, and there were no reports that government officials employed them.

Prison and Detention Center Conditions

High prison populations and overcrowding, poor sanitary conditions in some prisons, cases of mistreatment of inmates, and generally unsatisfactory conditions for inmates with physical or mental disabilities remained the main concerns during the year.

The situation in migrant detention facilities improved significantly during the year as the number of migrants from the Middle East, Africa, and Asia entering the country dramatically decreased. Children stayed with their families in one detention facility for irregular migrants but were able to leave the facility accompanied by staff.

Physical Conditions: Prison overcrowding was a problem. While an amnesty in 2013 temporarily relieved overcrowding, it did not improve services to prisoners, since the government cut prison staff proportionally. Facilities for prisoners serving their sentences were at almost 107 percent of capacity in the first seven months of the year.

There were 20 deaths in prisons and detention facilities in the first half of the year. There was no information available on the causes of those deaths.

In her *Report on Systematic Visits to Prisons* for the year, the public defender of rights (ombudswoman) reported mistreatment of inmates in two prisons and generally unsatisfactory conditions of imprisonment for convicts with physical or mental disabilities. She also criticized the prison health-care system, whose inadequate standards she blamed on the lack of physicians motivated to work in prisons.

Prisoners had limited access to hot water, which posed sanitary problems.

<u>Administration</u>: Authorities permitted prisoners and detainees to submit complaints to the ombudswoman without censorship, and the ombudswoman investigated credible allegations of inhuman conditions and made routine prison visits. According to the Ministry of Justice and the ombudsman, prisoners were allowed appropriate access to visitors and opportunities for religious observances. The Ministry of Justice, which oversees the prison system, inspected prisons throughout the year.

<u>Independent Monitoring</u>: The government permitted independent monitoring of prison conditions by local and international human rights groups, such as the Helsinki Commission and the Council of Europe's Committee for the Prevention of Torture (CPT), and by the media.

<u>Improvements</u>: In her report the ombudswoman noted that the Prison Service had accepted her proposal to establish a transparent system for relocating convicts to prisons closer to their homes.

d. Arbitrary Arrest or Detention

The law prohibits arbitrary arrest and detention, and the government generally observed these prohibitions.

Role of the Police and Security Apparatus

The national police, who report to the Ministry of Interior, are responsible for enforcing the law and maintaining public order, including protecting the border and enforcing the immigration law. The General Inspectorate of Security Forces (GIBS), which reports to the Office of the Prime Minister, oversees police, customs, fire fighters, and the prison service and is responsible for investigating allegations of misconduct. Inspectors investigated allegations of criminal misconduct and carried out "integrity tests," or sting operations, to catch violators in action. In 2015 inspectors opened proceedings in 276 cases nationwide. Authorities reported that police committed 232 crimes in 2015, an increase of 120 since 2014, while members of the prison service committed 29 crimes, an increase of 11. Customs officers committed 12 crimes, compared with 11 in 2014.

Corruption remained a problem among law enforcement bodies. In 2015 police investigated 174 cases of corruption, compared with 116 cases in 2014. Police also investigated 73 public figures for abuse of power. In August the municipal court in Tabor sentenced the former head of Litomerice prison, Tomas Libal, to three years' probation and fined him 100,000 koruna ($4,100) for corruption and extortion.

The Ministry of Interior has a police ombudswoman who serves as a mediator within the ministry. All public safety personnel, including civilians, employed by the ministry can approach the ombudswoman with suspicions of possible wrongdoing or improper activities. Police ombudswoman focuses primarily on prevention, transparency, and repression. In cases of suspected criminal misconduct, she forwards the case to the GIBS, which investigates police officers. The law requires police ombudsman to share all information about cases with GIBS upon request, which led to privacy and confidentiality concerns.

Arrest Procedures and Treatment of Detainees

In most cases police use judicial warrants to arrest persons accused of criminal acts. Police may make arrests without a warrant when they believe a prosecutable offense has been committed, when they regard arrest as necessary to prevent further offenses or the destruction of evidence, to protect a suspect, or when a person refuses to obey police orders to move.

Police must refer persons arrested on a warrant to a court within 24 hours. A judge has an additional 24 hours to decide whether to continue to hold the individuals. For suspects arrested without a warrant, police have 48 hours to inform them of the reason for the arrest, question them, and either release them or refer them to a court, after which a judge must decide within 24 hours whether to charge them. Authorities may not hold detainees for a longer period without charge.

The law provides for bail except in cases of serious crimes or to prevent witness tampering. A defendant in a criminal case may request a lawyer immediately upon arrest. If a defendant cannot afford a lawyer, the government provides one. The court determines whether the government partially or fully covers attorneys' fees. Authorities generally respected these rights.

In August the district court in Sokolov acquitted two police officers on trial since 2014 for negligence in the 2012 death of a Romani man held in custody. According to witnesses, the officers beat the man after they arrested him at the home of his estranged wife. The verdict relied on the autopsy, which identified the man's cause of death as delirium tremens. The court's decision was final.

<u>Pretrial Detention</u>: By law pretrial detention may last no longer than two years except for exceptionally grave offenses. A suspect may petition investigating authorities at any time for release. In the first six months of the year, the average length of pretrial detention was 61 days.

<u>Detainee's Ability to Challenge Lawfulness of Detention before a Court</u>: Persons detained or arrested on criminal or other grounds were entitled to challenge in court the legal basis or arbitrary nature of their detention and obtain prompt release/compensation if found to have been unlawfully detained.

e. Denial of Fair Public Trial

The law provides for an independent judiciary, and the government generally respected judicial independence. In most instances authorities respected court orders and carried out judicial decisions.

Trial Procedures

The law provides for the right to a fair public trial, and an independent judiciary generally enforced this right.

Defendants enjoy the right to a presumption of innocence and the right to receive prompt and detailed information about the charges against them (with free interpretation as necessary). They have the right to a fair and public trial without undue delay, the right to be present at their trial, and the right to communicate with an attorney of their choice or have one provided at public expense if they are unable to pay. They generally have adequate time and facilities to prepare a defense and have the right to free interpretation as necessary from the moment charged through all appeals. Defendants have access to government-held evidence, have the right to confront prosecution or plaintiff witnesses and present their own witnesses and evidence. They cannot be compelled to testify or confess guilt. Convicted persons have a right of appeal. The law extends the above rights to all defendants.

Political Prisoners and Detainees

There were no reports of political prisoners or detainees.

Civil Judicial Procedures and Remedies

The constitution provides for a separate, independent judiciary in civil matters and for lawsuits seeking damages for, or cessation of, human rights violations. Available remedies include monetary damages, equitable relief, and cessation of harmful conduct. NGOs reported increased coherence between criminal and civil procedures that simplified the process for victims. At times, however, remedies and relief still required a lengthy legal process and were difficult to obtain, particularly for members of disadvantaged groups, such as the Romani minority. Plaintiffs may appeal unfavorable rulings that involve alleged violations of the European Convention on Human Rights to the European Court of Human Rights. Administrative remedies are also available.

The law recognizes children, persons with disabilities, victims of human trafficking, and victims of sexual and brutal crimes as the most vulnerable populations. It lists the rights of crime victims, such as to claim compensation and have access to an attorney. Victims of sexual crimes may choose the gender of the judge who will preside over the trials of their alleged assailants.

Property Restitution

The law provides for restitution of private property confiscated under the communist regime as well as restitution of, or compensation for, Jewish property seized during the Nazi era. Although it was still possible during the year to file claims for artwork confiscated by the Nazi regime, the claims period for other types of property had expired. The law allows for restitution and compensation for property of religious organizations, including Jewish religious communities, confiscated under the communist regime. Within the one-year period stipulated by the law, churches filed 7,445 claims. Churches are also to receive compensation of 59 billion korunas ($2.4 billion) for property that is not returnable. The law provides that the state pay compensation over a period of 30 years while simultaneously phasing out state subsidies for registered religious groups over a 17-year period.

f. Arbitrary or Unlawful Interference with Privacy, Family, Home, or Correspondence

The law prohibits such actions, and there were no reports that the government failed to respect these prohibitions.

In June the Prague District Court acquitted Jana Necasova, the wife and then chief of staff of former prime minister Petr Necas, as well as three military intelligence officers, of charges of corruption and unwarranted surveillance of Necas's former wife. The prosecutor appealed the decision, and the case will go again before the Prague Municipal Court. If convicted, Necasova faces up to three-and-a-half years in prison.

Section 2. Respect for Civil Liberties, Including:

a. Freedom of Speech and Press

The law provides for freedom of speech and press, and the government generally respected these rights. An independent press, an effective judiciary, and a functioning democratic political system combined to promote freedom of speech and press. The law provides for some limitations to this freedom, including in cases of hate speech, Holocaust denial, and denial of communist-era crimes.

Freedom of Speech and Expression: The law mandates prison sentences of six months to three years for persons who deny communist-era crimes or the Holocaust. The law prohibits speech that incites hatred based on race, religion, class, nationality, or other group affiliation and provides for prison sentences of up to three years for violations.

Press and Media Freedoms: Independent media were active and expressed a wide variety of views without government restriction but there was a reported instance of a private media outlet restricting its reporters. Investigations by an NGO revealed that management of Prima TV, the third-most-watched television station in the country, instructed its reporters to present the migration crisis only as a threat and to focus on concern about Islamization and the danger posed by refugees. Management reportedly announced that anyone who did not follow this approach would not be able to work at Prima. Several legislators publicly criticized Prima TV.

The law providing limitations on denial of communist-era crimes and the Holocaust and on hate speech applies to the print and broadcast media as well as online newspapers and journals.

Internet Freedom

The government did not restrict or disrupt access to the internet or censor online content, and there were no credible reports that the government monitored private online communications without appropriate legal authority. According to current data from the Czech Statistical Office, over 73 percent of households used high-speed internet during the year.

Authorities were increasingly willing to prosecute hate speech on the internet, although extremists often stymied their efforts by placing their pages on foreign servers beyond the reach of authorities. One website, hosted abroad but run by Slovak white supremacists, listed the names and addresses of many Czech lesbian, gay, bisexual, transgender, and intersex (LGBTI) persons as well as Romani activists and advocates. In some cases the supremacists hacked webpages, such as that of the Czech Helsinki Committee, and called for violence against individuals, such as the director of a major Romani NGO. In 2015 the courts fined several websites for publishing or allowing hate speech in internet discussions.

Academic Freedom and Cultural Events

There were no government restrictions on academic freedom or cultural events.

b. Freedom of Peaceful Assembly and Association

Freedom of Assembly

The constitution and law provides for the freedom of assembly, and the government generally respected this right. The government may legally restrict or prohibit gatherings, including marches, demonstrations, and concerts, if they promote hatred or intolerance, advocate suppressing individual rights, or jeopardize the safety of participants.

In May the Municipal Court in Prague received a complaint by citizens who wanted to stage a protest demonstration against the violation of human rights in China during the visit of the president of China to Prague in March. While the demonstration was announced to authorities as required by law, police banned it upon the decision of the Prague municipality, allegedly for security reasons. The complainants claimed that the constitutional right to assembly could not be restricted by a decree, but only under the law on assembly. The case was pending at year's end.

Freedom of Association

The constitution and law provide for freedom of association. While the government generally respected this right, the law requires organizations, associations, foundations, and political parties to register with the Ministry of Interior. The courts may dissolve or ban, and the Ministry of Interior may refuse to register, groups that incite hatred based on race, religion, class, nationality, or other affiliation or that use prohibited symbols.

c. Freedom of Religion

See the Department of State's *International Religious Freedom Report* at www.state.gov/religiousfreedomreport/.

d. Freedom of Movement, Internally Displaced Persons, Protection of Refugees, and Stateless Persons

The constitution and law provide for freedom of internal movement, foreign travel, emigration, and repatriation, and the government generally respected these rights.

Abuse of Migrants, Refugees, and Stateless Persons: Acts of physical intimidation, vandalism, and inflammatory antimigrant rhetoric related to the European migrant crisis remained a serious concern. NGOs focusing on migration issues reported an increase in telephone and e-mail threats, including death threats (see section 6, Other Societal Violence and Discrimination).

The government cooperated with the Office of the UN High Commissioner for Refugees (UNHCR) and other humanitarian organizations in providing protection and assistance to refugees, asylum seekers, stateless persons, and other persons of concern.

Protection of Refugees

Access to Asylum: The law provides for the granting of asylum or subsidiary protection, and the government has established a system for providing protection to refugees. According to Ministry of Interior statistics for the first half of the year, the length of asylum procedures met the requirements of the new Law on Asylum that entered into force on January 1. Under the new law, the Ministry of Interior should grant asylum within six months of the date the application if the applicant has submitted all required documents.

Safe Country of Origin/Transit: The country generally adheres to the Dublin III regulation, which calls for authorities to return refugees to the first EU country they entered. The Ministry of Interior accepted asylum applications from persons arriving from or through countries deemed to be safe, as defined by law. Authorities usually denied such applications but reviewed all cases individually.

<u>Freedom of Movement</u>: There were reports of long detentions of migrants and asylum seekers facing extradition or waiting for voluntary repatriation. According to a Ministry of Interior report in October, there were 107 migrants detained in three facilities in the country. Under the law migrants facing deportation or waiting for voluntary repatriation can be detained for a maximum of 180 days. If there are children accompanying the adults, the deportation procedure can last no more than 90 days. NGOs criticized the fact that children of migrants were placed in detention facilities together with their parents.

Several bar association members and NGO legal experts provided legal aid to migrants and had access to detention facilities. Independent observers had access to detention facilities.

<u>Durable Solutions</u>: A national resettlement and integration program managed by the government in close cooperation with UNHCR continued. Under the State Integration Plan approved by the government in November 2015, beneficiaries of international protection are entitled to temporary accommodation, social services, Czech language training, and assistance with finding employment and permanent housing. Children are entitled to school education. The country accepted Syrian asylum seekers beginning in October 2015, including four families with gravely ill children under the Medevac program. Most of them later left for Germany.

Following EU approval of a mechanism to relocate migrants and asylum seekers through mandatory quotas, the country relocated 12 Syrians from Greece in 2015. Additionally, under an agreement between the EU and Turkey, the government agreed to resettle 1,301 persons from Turkey and 400 refugees from other countries, mainly from the Middle East.

<u>Temporary Protection</u>: The government provided temporary (subsidiary) protection to individuals who do not satisfy the legal criteria for refugee status but who cannot return to their country of origin due to the risk of serious harm. Under EU guidelines, individuals granted subsidiary protection are eligible for temporary residence permits, travel documents, access to employment, equal access to health care and housing, and school education for children. The government provided temporary protection to 217 persons in the first six months of the year.

Stateless Persons

According to UNHCR, as of mid-2015 there were 1,502 persons in the country who fell under UNHCR's statelessness mandate. The Ministry of Interior reported 18 stateless persons that were also refugees who applied for international protection through June. Four of them were repeat applicants, 14 were women, and 11 were minors. Under certain circumstances, stateless persons can obtain citizenship.

Section 3. Freedom to Participate in the Political Process

The constitution and law provide citizens the ability to choose their government through free and fair periodic elections based on universal and equal suffrage and conducted by secret ballot to assure the free expression of the will of the people.

Elections and Political Participation

Recent Elections: In October authorities held elections for one-third of the seats in the senate and for regional government positions; a second round of senate elections was held later that month. There were no reports of any irregularities.

Participation of Women and Minorities: No laws limit the participation of women or members of minorities in the political process, and women and minorities did participate.

Roma participated in politics and were members of mainstream as well as Romani-specific political parties, although few of the country's estimated 300,000 socially excluded Roma were integrated into political life. There were no Romani members of parliament, cabinet ministers, or Supreme Court justices; in the regional elections, Romani candidates had no success winning office. There were some Romani appointees to national and regional advisory councils dealing with Romani affairs.

Section 4. Corruption and Lack of Transparency in Government

The law provides criminal penalties for corruption by officials. An offender may face a fine of up to 100 percent of funds embezzled and up to three years in prison if he does not cooperate with the tax office. The government generally implemented the law effectively, although officials sometimes engaged in corrupt practices with impunity.

<u>Corruption</u>: In May the High Court in Prague sentenced Marek Dalik, a lobbyist and former advisor to former prime minister Mirek Topolanek, to four years in prison and four million koruna ($163,000) in fines on charges of corruption. The case concerned the government's purchase of Pandur military armored vehicles from the Steyer Company. Dalik demanded 18 million euro ($20 million) from Steyer officials in exchange for mediating the purchase. Dalik started his prison sentence on September 1. Both Dalik and the supreme public prosecutor have filed special appeals.

<u>Financial Disclosure</u>: The law obliges legislators, members of the cabinet, and other selected public officials to declare their assets annually. The public can view the declarations on a website, but access remained difficult because it requires a time-sensitive password issued by the official's department. The information tended to be general and lacked detail.

<u>Public Access to Information</u>: The law provides for public access to government information, and in most cases the law was effectively implemented. NGOs reported inconsistent practices in releasing information, noting that authorities were reluctant to release information to the public proactively, especially concerning the salaries of public officials, public tenders, and other uses of public finances.

Section 5. Governmental Attitude Regarding International and Nongovernmental Investigation of Alleged Violations of Human Rights

A variety of domestic and international human rights groups generally operated without governmental restriction, investigating and publishing their findings on human rights cases. Government officials were generally cooperative and responsive to their views.

<u>Government Human Rights Bodies</u>: Representatives from the Office of the Public Defender of Rights (ombudswoman) made regular visits to government and private facilities where residents had limited movement (that is prisons, orphanages, senior citizens' homes, and detention facilities), examining the treatment of individuals and monitoring respect for their fundamental rights. The office issued quarterly and annual reports on its activities in addition to reports and recommendations on topics of special concern to the government. The office operated without government or party interference, had adequate resources, and human rights observers generally regarded it as effective. In its October 2015 report, however, the European Commission against Racism and Intolerance found that the

ombudswoman lacked sufficient power and responsibility to combat racial discrimination effectively.

In addition to the public defender of rights, there are ombudsmen for security forces and for education.

In 2014 the government re-established the position of human rights minister to pursue a domestic human rights agenda. The Office of the Government (the central body of state administration) supported several human rights-related councils.

Section 6. Discrimination, Societal Abuses, and Trafficking in Persons

Women

Rape and Domestic Violence: The law prohibits rape, including spousal rape, and provides a penalty of two to 15 years in prison for violations. The government effectively enforced these provisions. Although experts still considered rape underreported, they noted an upward trend in the number of rape convictions. They attributed this trend to improved police training, public awareness campaigns, and greater interaction between police and NGOs. In the first six months of the year, authorities recorded 325 rapes and adjudicated 195 of them. Courts convicted 134 offenders, 75 of whom received prison sentences; the remainder received suspended sentences.

Experts believed violence against women was more widespread than suggested by the number of cases reported to authorities due to the stigma associated with such abuses. NGOs noted in particular the underreporting of violence against women in immigrant communities, where victims often feared losing their immigration status or being subjected to cultural stigma. Some NGOs continued to offer increased social, legal, and psychological services to rape victims.

Domestic violence is punishable by up to three years in prison, with longer sentences in aggravated circumstances. Police have the authority to remove violent abusers from their homes for 10 days. The law limits to six months the total time, including extensions, a removal order can remain in effect. The NGO White Circle of Safety reported that, in the first six months of the year, police removed 672 offenders (some of them women) from their homes.

In the first six months of the year, the Ministry of Interior received 321 reported cases of domestic violence, and police investigated 211 cases. During the same period, courts convicted 116 individuals of domestic violence, sentencing 39 of them to prison terms. The courts issued suspended sentences to 76 persons convicted and put one under house arrest.

The law also provides protection against domestic violence to other persons living in the household, especially children and seniors, and allows legal emancipation for children from the age of 16 under certain circumstances. For example, a child may request a court order to remove an aggressor from the family in case a parent (usually the mother) was not willing or able to do so.

According to the Czech Psychiatric Society, 32 percent of women and 2.5 percent of men experienced domestic violence in the first half of the year. Research conducted by the ProFem society found that 28 percent of women experienced domestic violence and one third of them needed medical treatment. In 68 percent of cases, children witnessed domestic violence. The Ministry of Interior reported that all police officers undergo specialized training that focuses on the law on domestic violence, assistance to the victims, and other related issues.

Sexual Harassment: The antidiscrimination law prohibits sexual harassment and treats it as a form of direct discrimination. A person who has been harassed may seek justice through the courts and request compensation for possible harm. The burden of proof is on the accused party, who has to prove that he or she did not discriminate against the accuser. Penalties for conviction may include fines, dismissal from work, or imprisonment for up to eight years. Most cases of sexual harassment took place in the workplace. According to NGOs police rarely investigated such cases because victims usually preferred to seek advice on how to stop the harassment rather than accuse colleagues or supervisors and risk losing their jobs. Police often delayed investigations until the perpetrator committed serious crimes, such as sexual coercion, rape, or other forms of physical assault.

Offenders convicted of stalking may receive sentences of up to three years in prison. In the first six months of the year, police investigated 259 reports of stalking and adjudicated 164 of them. Police also cleared 49 cases from previous periods. In the first six months of the year, courts convicted 113 persons of stalking, of whom 12 received prison sentences, 89 received suspended sentences, and the others were fined or sentenced to community service. According to police statistics, 75 percent of the victims were women.

NGOs reported an increase in cyberbullying or cyberstalking, not only of children but also of adults of both sexes. In response to this rise, the NGOs Gender Studies and ProFem conducted a campaign against cyberbullying.

Reproductive Rights: The government recognized the basic right of couples and individuals to decide the number, spacing, and timing of their children; manage their reproductive health; and have access to the information and means to do so, free from discrimination, coercion, or violence.

In October the government rejected a bill proposed in September 2015 by the minister of human rights on compensation for persons, most of them Romani women, who were sterilized without their full consent between 1971 and 1991.

Discrimination: The law grants men and women the same legal status and rights, including under family, labor, property, nationality, and inheritance laws. Women sometimes experienced discrimination in the area of employment (see section 7.d.).

Children

Birth Registration: Children derive their citizenship from their parents. Any child with at least one citizen parent is automatically a citizen. Authorities registered births immediately.

Child Abuse: Although illegal, child abuse remained a problem. By law any person under the age of 18 is a minor. Additionally, a child is considered an endangered individual and regarded as a victim in cases of domestic violence, even if the violence does not specifically target the child.

NGOs estimated that 40,000 children experienced some form of violence every year. According to police and the Ministry of Interior, there were 751 cases of child abuse filed in 2015 and 432 cases filed in the first six months of the year, including sexual abuse and commercial sex exploitation. According to a report released by the Ministry of Labor and Social Affairs in April, the number of abused or mistreated children rose from 8,478 in 2014 to 9,433 in 2015. Six children died due to abuse or mistreatment in 2015. The Ministry of Labor and Social Affairs reported that in 2015 authorities removed 2,368 children from families and placed them in children's homes due to abuse or mistreatment.

Prison sentences for persons found guilty of child abuse range from five to 12 years in the case of the death of a child. The Ministries of Interior and Justice introduced special interviewing rooms for child victims and witnesses. A child victim is not required to give testimony in court when specially trained police officers have followed the correct procedures for interviewing the child, including having psychologists and, in some cases, judges and defense attorneys present.

Early and Forced Marriage: The minimum legal age for marriage is 18. Some members of the Romani community married before reaching legal age. The law allows for marriage at the age of 16 with court approval; no official marriages were reported of anyone under 16.

Sexual Exploitation of Children: The law prohibits commercial sexual exploitation of children and the possession, manufacture, and distribution of child pornography, which is punishable by imprisonment for up to eight years. The minimum age for consensual sex is 15. Sexual relations with a child younger than 15 is punishable by a prison term of up to eight years or up to 18 years in the case of the death of the child. The government prohibits all forms of trafficking under the criminal code, which prescribes punishments of up to 16 years' imprisonment for violations. According to Ministry of Interior statistics, police investigated 55 cases of commercial sexual exploitation of children in the first six months of the year, compared with 25 cases in 2015.

In the first six months of the year, the Ministry of Justice reported that courts convicted 41 individuals for production or handling of child pornography, two of whom received prison sentences of up to five years in prison, three received sentences of up to 15 years in prison, and the remaining 36 received suspended sentences. Courts convicted 17 individuals of misuse of a child for the production of pornography, five of who received prison sentences.

International Child Abductions: The country is a party to the 1980 Hague Convention on the Civil Aspects of International Child Abduction. See the Department of State's *Annual Report on International Parental Child Abduction* at travel.state.gov/content/childabduction/en/legal/compliance.html.

Anti-Semitism

The country's Jewish population numbers approximately 10,000. Public expressions of anti-Semitism were rare, but small, fairly well organized right-wing groups with anti-Semitic views were active around the country. The Ministry of Interior continued to monitor the activities of such groups, increase cooperation with police from neighboring countries, and shut their unauthorized rallies.

In 2015 the Ministry of Interior recorded 47 criminal offenses with anti-Semitic motives, compared to 45 in 2014. During the same period, the Federation of Jewish Communities reported 39 anti-Semitic incidents, including damage to property, spray painting of anti-Semitic slogans and Nazi symbols, threats, and harassment. The number of anti-Semitic articles written by Czechs on the internet, including incitement to violence against Jews, decreased from 191 in 2014 to 182 in 2015. A well-known anti-Semitic blogger continued his internet postings, including statements denying the Holocaust. In March he was put on probation and in April charged with incitement to hatred and Holocaust denial. The case was pending at year's end.

In July the Ministry of Culture designated a former Jewish cemetery in Prostejov as a cultural monument. The move invigorated a three-year effort, led by a foreign philanthropist, to restore the cemetery, which had been eradicated by the Nazis. After the war the site was turned into a public park. The local mayor opposed the restoration, claiming the park provided needed access to a nearby school and another part of the former cemetery was used for residential parking.

Trafficking in Persons

See the Department of State's *Trafficking in Persons Report* at www.state.gov/j/tip/rls/tiprpt/.

Persons with Disabilities

The law prohibits discrimination against persons with physical, sensory, intellectual, and mental disabilities in employment, education, public transportation services, access to health care, the judicial system, and the provision of other government services. The government generally enforced these provisions. Nevertheless, persons with disabilities faced a shortage of public accommodations and were unemployed at disproportionately high rates. Most children with disabilities were able to attend mainstream primary and secondary schools and universities.

In April the parliament passed an education law intended to reduce the use of special schools for children with mild disabilities and for certain minorities (including Roma). The law went into effect in September, and as a result over 200 first grade students with disabilities or from socially excluded localities enrolled in mainstream schools. According to the law, only children with significant disabilities should attend special schools with specially trained teachers.

The law requires a legal guardian to assure that the preferences of a person with a mental or psychological disability are considered. Courts cannot deprive such individuals of their full legal rights but may limit rights in some clearly specified areas (for example finances, the right to vote). Courts have three years to review cases of mentally or physically disabled persons with curtailed legal rights to determine whether the treatment of such individuals complies with the law.

The ombudswoman is required to make regular visits to all governmental and private workplaces employing incarcerated or institutionalized persons, including persons with disabilities, to examine conditions, assure respect for fundamental rights, and advocate for improved protection against mistreatment. The ombudswoman's office conducted such visits throughout the year. The ombudswoman cooperated with the Supreme Public Prosecutor to protect incarcerated or institutionalized persons.

According to a report by the Ministry for Human Rights, during 2015 government ministries were not complying with the law that requires 4 percent of the staff of companies and institutions with more than 25 employees to be persons with physical disabilities. According to the report, only three of 25 government ministries and their branches met the requirement. Instead of employing persons with disabilities, many companies and institutions paid fines or bought products from companies that employed persons with disabilities, a practice that the National Disability Council criticized.

The Ministry of Labor and Social Affairs continued an EU-funded program to assist persons with disabilities in transitioning from institutional care into mainstream society.

National/Racial/Ethnic Minorities

The approximately 300,000 Roma in the country faced varying levels of discrimination in education, employment, and housing and have high levels of poverty, unemployment, and illiteracy. A series of public opinion polls reflected societal prejudice. A poll conducted by the Center for Research of Public Opinion (CVVM) in March, for example, found that 82 percent of respondents considered Roma "unlikeable" or "very unlikeable," while only 3 percent had compassion for Roma and 14 percent had neutral opinions. A 2015 poll conducted by the

European Commission found that only 29 percent of Czechs would feel comfortable or indifferent about working with a Romani person and only 11 percent would feel comfortable or indifferent if their child fell in love with a Rom. The same poll indicated negative attitudes towards certain perceived attributes of Asians and blacks.

According to research data published by the NGO In Iusticia, there were 10 ethnically motivated violent incidents recorded in the first half of 2015, four of which were directed against Roma. According to the Ministry of Interior, Roma were the victims of 33 various criminal acts in 2015.

According to the Ministry of Interior's 2015 *Report on Extremism*, there were 175 hate crimes reported during that year for which 130 persons were prosecuted and 115 charged. Two persons were sentenced to one to five years in prison, one person was sentenced to one year in prison, 37 persons were put on probation, and nine were sentenced to community work.

In June, two defendants were sentenced to over six years in prison for attempted murder in connection with their racially motivated attack against Roma in 2012. The case is pending because of an appeal. Regional police were investigating an August incident in which an armed man intimidated Czech and Slovak Romani children attending a summer camp. In February a dentist who refused to treat a Romani man and his daughter was ordered by a court to apologize in writing and to pay compensation to her victims.

A white supremacist webpage registered outside the country, listed the names and addresses of Romani activists and hacked the website and e-mail addresses of several high-profile individuals who either worked on Romani issues or expressed support for Roma in the past.

During the year the deputy prime minister and finance minister came under criticism for stating (incorrectly) that the World War II-era Lety concentration camp for Roma was only a camp for those unwilling to work. He later apologized and corrected his statement.

A high number of Romani children attended special schools, which effectively segregated them into a substandard educational system.

Approximately one-third of Roma lived in "excluded localities" or ghettos. According to an October 2015 report by the Ministry for Labor and Social Affairs, the number of ghettos doubled to 606 since 2006, and their population grew from 80,000 to 115,000. Ghettos usually have substandard housing and poor health conditions.

NGOs examined multiple housing advertisements and found that Romani applicants experienced discrimination when seeking to rent residential or business properties. While the law prohibits housing discrimination based on ethnicity, NGOs stated that some municipalities discriminated against certain socially disadvantaged groups, primarily Roma, basing their decisions not to supply housing on the allegedly bad reputation of Romani applicants from previous residences. Other examples of discrimination against Romani consumers also included failure to serve them food in restaurants and a refusal to accommodate Roma in a motel. Roma were disproportionally subject to indebtedness due to lack of access to banking services and exploitation by predatory lenders.

The Agency for Social Inclusion is responsible for implementing the government's strategy to combat social exclusion mainly among the Romani population; to improve access to education, housing, security, and family, social, and health services; and to stimulate regional development of most affected areas. The minister for human rights and the minister for labor and social affairs also made public statements in support of socially disadvantaged groups, in particular Roma, and advocated policies favorable to them within the government.

Acts of Violence, Discrimination, and Other Abuses Based on Sexual Orientation and Gender Identity

The country has antidiscrimination laws that cover sexual orientation. In its report published in October 2015, the European Commission against Racial Intolerance criticized the country for not having specific hate crime provisions covering sexual orientation and gender identity.

The government did not keep statistics on incidents of violence directed at individuals based on their sexual orientation or gender identity, but NGO contacts reported the number of such incidents was very low. Local LGBTI activists stated that citizens were largely tolerant of LGBTI persons. A June opinion poll by the CVVM, for example, found that 74 percent of respondents agreed that gays and lesbians should have the right to enter a registered partnership. The same poll found that 37 percent of respondents said they had friends in the LGBTI community. According to the poll, 48 percent of respondents believed that "coming out" would cause problems for them in their town or village.

According to a survey conducted by the EU Agency for Fundamental Rights, 36 percent of LGBTI persons reported experiencing discrimination and harassment due to their sexual orientation, while 26 percent reported they had been physically attacked or threatened over the previous five years.

In July, Pavlina Nytrova, Czech Social Democratic Party parliamentarian, speaking against adoptions by LGBTI persons, stated that such persons are highly promiscuous, have above-average rates of alcohol abuse and drug addiction, and will want to legalize sex with children. The comment caused an uproar and the labor minister (also a Social Democrat) suggested Nytrova resign from the party.

Some health care measures, such as in vitro fertilization, are available only to heterosexual couples.

In June the Constitutional Court struck down a ban on gay and lesbian persons living in registered partnerships from adopting children as individuals. Joint adoption by same-sex couples and adoption of a same-sex partner's biological child, however, remains illegal.

HIV and AIDS Social Stigma

Persons with HIV/AIDS faced societal discrimination, although there were no reported cases of violence. The Czech AIDS Help Society reported a number of cases of discrimination, primarily in access to health and dental care and wrongful termination of employment or discrimination during the hiring process. The government took no action in most cases, since individuals with HIV/AIDS often preferred to keep their status confidential rather than file a complaint. In the first half of the year, the ombudswoman's office delivered a number of presentations at national events concerning the status of HIV infection as a disability under the antidiscrimination law. The ombudswoman also criticized an amendment to the Protection of Public Health Act over concerns that it promoted stigmatization and discrimination against individuals who are HIV-positive.

In March the District Court in Prague opened the case of a former police officer who was dismissed from work five years earlier because he was HIV-positive. The officer asked for financial compensation of 500,000 koruna ($20,400) from the Ministry of Interior. The judge requested expert medical evidence on whether the officer was capable of performing his duty despite his health condition. The case was pending at year's end.

Other Societal Violence and Discrimination

Societal prejudice and discrimination against Muslims remained a growing concern. NGOs focusing on migration issues reported an increase in telephone and e-mail threats over the previous year, including, in a few cases, death threats.

In the first half of the year, the Ministry of Interior reported 88 extremist criminal acts, 64 of which were considered acts of violence or instigation to violence mainly against Muslims. The authorities prosecuted 50 of those cases.

Throughout the year there were several demonstrations against accepting migrants and refugees and against the EU for imposing resettlement quotas. The groups Anti-Islam Bloc, Usvit (Dawn), and We Don't Want Islam in Czech Republic organized most of the demonstrations, which drew between several dozen and 1,000 participants. There were also several demonstrations in support of migrants and refugees.

In February demonstrators against Islam threw Molotov cocktails at the "Klinika" social center in Prague. In April several cafes and shops in Prague that were part of a government "hate-free zone" project were sprayed with written threats and Nazi symbols. Police charged five youths in connection with this vandalism.

In July more than 60 neo-Nazis and other extremists demonstrated against a xenophobia awareness event in Ostrava. German Chancellor Angela Merkel's August visit to Prague prompted several demonstrations in support of and critical of her policies regarding refugees and migration. The anti-Merkel gatherings were more heavily attended; criticism focused on her welcoming refugees to Europe.

In August members of We Don't Want Islam in Czech Republic staged a fake Da'esh attack in Prague's Old Town Square. Members of the group dressed as terrorists with fake beards, fake suicide vests, and fake shotguns and rode into the square in military vehicles and on a camel, yelling, and firing noisemaker guns. The event was meant to be a stunt but caused panic. Dozens of tourists knocked over tables and chairs as they fled before police interrupted and terminated the demonstration.

Also in August an unknown perpetrator broke windows in the mosque in Brno, and in November someone poured motor oil on the mosque's doors and walls. No organization claimed responsibility for these incidents, and police continued to investigate the cases.

On September 11, approximately 25 persons staged a demonstration outside the Saudi Embassy in Prague dressed in Arab garments and mocking Islamic traditions.

NGOs reported an increase in the level of hate speech related to migration. Politicians, including the president, the deputy prime minister, members of parliament, senators, and local politicians across the political spectrum, used antimigrant rhetoric with Muslims the main target.

Although the government publicly condemned anti-Islamic rhetoric, President Zeman stated he would be in favor of deploying water cannons against migrants if the migration crisis reached the Czech border. Prime Minister Sobotka criticized President Zeman, asserting that water cannons were not a solution to the crisis. In October Zeman described migration as an organized invasion and suggested migrants be relocated to Africa or uninhabited Greek islands. The foreign minister responded, stating that such a proposal did not reflect the country's foreign policy. Deputy Prime Minister/Finance Minister Babis said repeatedly that Muslim refugees cannot be integrated, and the country should not receive any Muslim refugees.

NGOs actively worked to combat these attitudes, and several events promoting tolerance took place during the year. In August approximately 80 Muslims assembled in front of a Catholic Church in Prague to protest the growing incidence of violence in Europe. They symbolically attended mass at the church, staying quietly in the back. After the mass approximately 400 attendees, including Muslims, condemned terrorism and formed a human chain around the church.

The Agency for Social Inclusion is responsible for implementing the government's strategy for combating social exclusion, mainly among the Romani population, to improve access to education, housing, security, as well as family, social, and health services, and to stimulate regional development of most affected areas. The minister for human rights and the minister for labor and social affairs made public statements in support of socially disadvantaged groups, in particular Roma, and advocated policies favorable to them within the government.

Section 7. Worker Rights

a. Freedom of Association and the Right to Collective Bargaining

The law provides for the right of workers to form and join independent unions of their choice without authorization or excessive requirements. It permits them to conduct their activities without interference. The right to associate freely covers both citizens and foreign workers, but the latter generally did not join unions due to the often short-term nature of their employment or the lack of social interaction with employees who were citizens.

The law provides for collective bargaining. It prohibits antiunion discrimination and does not recognize union activity as a valid reason for dismissal. Workers in most occupations have the legal right to strike if mediation efforts fail, and they generally exercised this right.

Strikes can be restricted or prohibited in essential service sectors, including hospitals, electricity and water supply services, air traffic control, nuclear energy, and the oil and natural gas sector. Members of the armed forces, prosecutors, and judges may not form or join trade unions or strike. The scope for collective bargaining was limited for civil servants, whose wages were regulated by law. Only trade unions may legally represent workers, including nonmembers. When planning a strike, unions are required to inform employers in writing of the number of strikers and provide a list of the members of the strike committee or contact persons for negotiation. They must announce the strike at least three days in advance. While regulations entitle union members to conduct some union activities during work hours, they do not specify how much time workers may use for this purpose, leaving room for diverse interpretations on the part of employers.

The law protects union officials from dismissal by an employer during their term of union service and for 12 months after its completion. To dismiss a union official, an employer must seek prior consent from the employee's unit within the union. If the union does not consent, a dismissal notice is invalid.

The government worked to enforce such laws effectively and permitted unions to conduct their activities without interference. Government resources for inspections and remediation were adequate, and legal penalties in the form of fines were sufficient to deter violations.

The Czech-Moravian Federation of Trade Unions (CMKOS) complained that, under the law, employers are not required to consult with unions on matters related to individual employees or to seek mutual agreement on some workplace problems, hurting the ability of employees of small enterprises to maintain union rights.

According to CMKOS employer violations of the labor law and trade union rules increased during the year, following the trend of the previous several years. CMKOS reported a number of violations and cases of discrimination, including employers raising administrative obstacles to collective bargaining; making unauthorized, unilateral wage changes; and threatening to dismiss employees who asserted their union rights, refused to terminate union activities, or attempted to form unions.

According to CMKOS some employers forced employees to work without a regular work agreement during a "trial period," paying them only a minimum wage with the remaining amount provided "under the table" or not paying wages on time in violation of the labor law. Nevertheless, proving a violation of the law was difficult. Employees, union as well as nonunion, were often unwilling to file formal complaints or testify against their employers due to fear of losing their jobs, having their wages reduced, or being moved to positions with poorer working conditions. Employees would usually file complaints only if their jobs were immediately threatened or after a job loss.

According to CMKOS employees were making more inquiries regarding their trade union rights and ways to establish a trade union. CMKOS still reported cases of employers not allowing union members sufficient paid time off to fulfill their union responsibilities or pressuring union members to resign their employment to weaken the local union unit. There were cases of bullying of union officials, including unreasonable performance evaluation criteria, excessive monitoring of work performance, and being targeted for disciplinary action or reduced financial compensation based solely on union participation.

During the year labor unions most frequently used strike alerts and strikes to advance their goals. Strikes and strike alerts targeted wages, premium pay for overtime, concerns about the closure of a business without a follow-on social program, including reasonable compensation for disadvantaged employees such as single parent employees, or intended layoffs.

b. Prohibition of Forced or Compulsory Labor

The law prohibits all forms of forced or compulsory labor, and the government effectively enforced these prohibitions. In the previous few years, inspections were more numerous and enforcing the law was more effective.

The government implemented legislation tightening regulation of potentially abusive labor agencies by raising requirements to enter the labor agency business, levying fines for illegal employment, and establishing limits on temporary employment of foreign nationals. Resources, inspections, and remediation were adequate. Penalties for violations, which include financial penalties and/or license revocation, were sufficient to deter violations.

There were reports that men and women, including migrant workers, were subjected to forced labor, typically through debt bondage. The Ministry of Interior reported 17 victims of forced labor in the first 11 months of the year. Private labor agencies often used deceptive practices to recruit workers from abroad as well as from inside the country.

Also see the Department of State's *Trafficking in Persons Report* at www.state.gov/j/tip/rls/tiprpt/.

c. Prohibition of Child Labor and Minimum Age for Employment

The minimum age for employment is 15. Employment of children between the ages of 15 and 18 was subject to strict safety standards, limitations on hours of work, and the requirement that work not interfere with education. The law permits children to be employed only in certain areas: cultural and artistic activities, advertising, product promotion, and certain modelling and sport activities. Child labor is allowed only if a child obtains a positive health assessment from a pediatrician and prior approval by the Labor Office. A work permit for a child is issued for 12 months. Resources, inspections, and remediation were adequate. Infringement of child labor rules is subject to fines of up to two million koruna ($81,000). The State Bureau for Labor Inspections (SBLI) effectively enforced these regulations. During the year the SBLI did not report any child labor law violations.

d. Discrimination with Respect to Employment and Occupation

Labor laws and regulations prohibit any kind of discrimination based on nationality, race, color, religion, political opinion, national origin, sex, sexual orientation or gender identity, age, disability, HIV-positive status or presence of other communicable diseases, social status, or trade union membership. According to the 2015 analysis of socially excluded localities in Czech Republic conducted by the Gabal Analysis Company, unemployment within the Roma community is high, especially in socially excluded localities where it amounts to 80-85 percent. In the rest of the country, Romani unemployment was 39 percent, while among the non-Roma the rate was 6 percent.

In 2015 the SBLI conducted 336 checks for unequal treatment and discrimination. It imposed fines totaling 2.4 million koruna ($100,000) for violations of discrimination laws, mostly noncompliance with the requirement to employ a specific number of persons with disabilities, discrimination based on gender and age, or the publication of discriminatory job advertisements. According to CMKOS cases of labor discrimination usually involved gender pay gaps. Penalties for violation of employment discrimination laws include reinstatement and financial penalties.

According to the Czech Statistical Office, 3.3 percent of women were unemployed, compared with 2.9 percent of men. In 2015 women made up 44 percent of the nonagricultural workforce. Women's salaries lagged behind those of men by approximately 24 percent. In 2015 the ombudswoman received 379 complaints of discrimination in employment.

Associations supporting HIV-positive individuals reported cases of discrimination. HIV-positive individuals are not legally obligated to report their diagnoses to their employer unless the diagnosis prevents them from executing their duties. Some employers dismissed HIV-positive employees due to prejudices of other employees. To avoid accusations of discrimination, employers justified such dismissals on administrative grounds, such as redundancy.

The government generally enforced the antidiscrimination laws involving employment effectively by seeking the imposition of fines. According to the ombudsman's report, discrimination occurred in job advertisements, which mentioned criteria such as age, gender, physical disability, and nationality. Employees were often unwilling to file formal complaints or testify against their employers due to fear of losing their jobs, having their wages reduced, or being moved to positions with poorer working conditions.

e. Acceptable Conditions of Work

The Ministry of Labor and Social Affairs establishes and enforces minimum wage standards. In 2015 the national minimum wage increased from 9,200 to 9,900 koruna (from $375 to $403) per month. The "minimum subsistence cost," defined as the minimum amount needed to satisfy the basic needs of a working age adult for a month, was 2,200 koruna ($90). Enforcement of the minimum wage was one of the primary objectives of SBLI inspections.

The law provides for a 40-hour workweek, two days of rest per week, and a break of at least 30 minutes during the standard eight-hour workday. Employees are entitled to at least 20 days of paid annual leave. Employers may require up to eight hours per week of overtime to meet increased demand but not more than 150 hours of overtime in a calendar year. Additional overtime is subject to the consent of the employee. The labor code requires premium pay for overtime that is equal to at least 125 percent of average earnings.

The government set occupational health and safety standards. The labor code obliges an employer to provide safety and health protection in the workplace, maintain a safe and healthy work environment, and prevent health and safety risks.

SBLI inspectors conducted 6,801 checks for compliance with the labor code. The SBLI imposed fines totaling 14.4 million koruna ($590,000) for substantial violations involving contracts, wages, overtime pay, working hours, and rest periods. In 2015 there were 334 labor inspectors for occupational health and safety standards in the country. SBLI's labor inspection plan focused on sectors where there were typically high-risk working conditions, such as construction, agriculture, and forestry.

The SBLI is responsible for combating illegal employment. Labor inspectors prioritized inspections for illicit employment in those sectors that were especially vulnerable to illegal employment, such as the lodging/catering, retail, warehousing and logistic centers, agricultural, forestry, and construction industries. Inspectors conducted numerous inspections in selected, seasonal businesses, including outdoor swimming parks, ski resorts, gasoline stations, and service stations. To strengthen the effectiveness of inspections, SBLI inspectors acted in conjunction with the Labor Office, the Social Insurance Bureau, the Licensing Office, foreign police, the Customs Office, and police. In 2015 they conducted 9,583 inspections and imposed fines equal to 16 million koruna ($652,000) for substantial violations of labor laws involving illegal employment, contracts and wages, denied salary bonus payments, working hours and rest periods, and residency and working permits.

In 2015 the SBLI conducted 539 checks in work agencies employing migrant workers. According to the SBLI, the inspections revealed inconsistencies in work agreements, denials of salary bonus payments or on-time salary payments, as well as inconsistencies involving working hours, overtime, and breaks. For substantial infringements of the labor law, the SBLI imposed 158 fines totaling 4.2 million koruna ($171,000). Although the SBLI did not find any cases of systematic discrimination based on citizenship, gender, age, or health status, violations were most frequently reported in cases where labor and wage conditions for permanent staff differed from those of temporary workers hired by agencies.

Employers sometimes ignored standard work conditions requirements in situations involving migrant workers. Over 90 percent of migrant workers were Ukrainians. Migrant workers were most frequently employed in the construction industry and forestry. Many of them worked in the so-called shadow economy with no work permits and often faced hazardous and exploitative working conditions. Relatively unskilled foreign workers from less developed countries were sometimes dependent on temporary employment agencies to find and retain work. Migrants sometimes worked in substandard conditions and were subjected to undignified treatment by these agencies. Most commonly, salaries were paid to the agencies, which then garnished them, resulting in workers receiving subminimum wages, working overtime without proper compensation, or working without compensation. Since migrant workers seldom filed formal complaints of such abuses, authorities had few opportunities to intervene.

The SBLI effectively enforced health and safety standards. Laws requiring acceptable conditions of work cover all workers equally in all sectors. During the year the SBLI conducted 10,608 checks focused on health and safety standards, primarily in the construction, manufacturing, transportation, agricultural, forestry, and heavy machine industries. The inspections occurred both proactively and in response to complaints. Authorities imposed fines totaling 6.6 million korunas $269,000 in cases where infringement of the law was substantial.

In 2015 the number of registered injuries in the workplace increased by 2.8 percent from 2014. Fatal accidents increased by 12 percent during 2015. The vast majority of workplace injuries and deaths occurred in the mining, transport, construction, warehousing, and processing industries. According to the SBLI, the most common causes of injuries or fatal incidents included underestimated risk, falls from height, irresponsible application of dangerous work procedures and techniques, unauthorized conduct and/or stay in hazardous zones, and failure to observe bans. Employees of small and medium-sized companies often declined to use protective gear even though their employer provided it.

Workers may remove themselves from situations that endanger their health or safety without jeopardy to their employment, and the SBLI aimed to enforce this standard consistently.

www.ingramcontent.com/pod-product-compliance
Lightning Source LLC
Chambersburg PA
CBHW081257250726
48654CB00012B/1641